Funny Cars

BY DENNY VON FINN

BELLWETHER MEDIA • MINNEAPOLIS, MN

Are you ready to take it to the extreme?
Torque books thrust you into the action-packed world of sports, vehicles, and adventure. These books may include dirt, smoke, fire, and dangerous stunts.

WARNING: READ AT YOUR OWN RISK.

This edition first published in 2009 by Bellwether Media, Inc.

No part of this publication may be reproduced in whole or in part without written permission of the publisher. For information regarding permission, write to Bellwether Media, Inc., Attention: Permissions Department, 5357 Penn Avenue South, Minneapolis, MN 55419.

Library of Congress Cataloging-in-Publication Data
Von Finn, Denny.
  Funny cars / by Denny Von Finn.
    p. cm. — (Torque. Cool rides)
  Includes bibliographical references and index.
  Summary: "Full color photography accompanies engaging information about funny cars. The combination of high-interest subject matter and light text is intended for students in grades 3 through 7"—Provided by publisher.
  ISBN-13: 978-1-60014-255-0 (hardcover : alk. paper)
  ISBN-10: 1-60014-255-9 (hardcover : alk. paper)
  1. Funny cars—Juvenile literature. I. Title.

TL236.23.V66 2009
629.228--dc22   2008035641

Text copyright © 2009 by Bellwether Media, Inc.

Contents

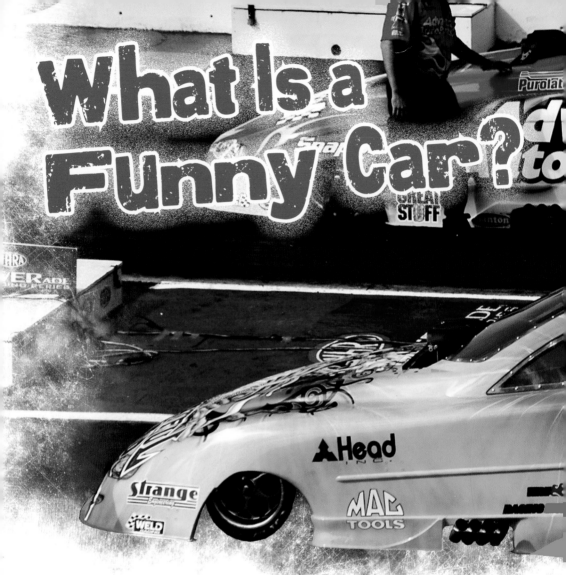

What Is a Funny Car?

A funny car is a vehicle designed for short races called drag races. In a drag race, two cars race in a straight line. Modern funny cars can travel at speeds of more than 300 miles (480 kilometers) per hour. Drag races last only a few seconds. The track is just a quarter-mile (0.4 kilometer) long.

Fast FaCt

A funny car needs up to 15 gallons (57 liters) of fuel for a single quarter-mile race.

Funny cars got their name when people began to **modify** Chrysler and Ford cars. The modifications, such as large rear tires, gave the cars a strange look. Funny cars got their name because of this look. Today's funny cars feature even more extreme modifications. They look nothing like normal cars on the street.

Funny Car History

Funny cars were developed in the 1960s. Drivers experimented with lightweight parts, which can give a car a good **power-to-weight ratio**. A great power-to-weight ratio can help a car go much faster. Good **traction** can also make a car faster. Custom carmakers shortened the **wheelbase** of funny cars to give them better traction.

Fast Fact

In 2008, Ashley Force became the first woman to win a national funny car race.

Today's top [...]
National Hot Rod Assoc[...]
NHRA was formed to promote safe [...]

Drivers also experimented to make funny cars faster. "Dyno" Don Nicholson was an early funny car builder and driver. In 1965, he began using **nitromethane** for fuel. He was the first driver whose car had a body that flipped up. Both of these changes made funny cars faster. Today, all funny cars burn nitromethane and have flip-up bodies.

Parts Of a Funny Car

The base of a funny car is its **chassis**. This is a frame of metal tubing that supports the body, engine, and other parts. The tubing is lightweight, but strong enough to withstand forces created by the engine.

chassis

The engine of a funny car is mounted to the chassis. The engine sits in front of the driver. A **supercharger** mixes large amounts of air with nitromethane fuel to create an incredible amount of **horsepower**. Today's funny car engines produce 7,000 horsepower! That's more than 30 times as much as a typical automobile engine.

The power from the engine is sent to the **driveshaft**. The driveshaft then transfers the power to the rear wheels. The funny car's rear tires are up to 17 inches (43 centimeters) wide.

A sleek body covers the engine, chassis, and driver of a funny car. The body must resemble the body of a **production vehicle**. Bodies are lightweight and made of **carbon fiber**. The driver climbs into the seat when the body is flipped up.

Funny Cars in Action

Before a race, drivers speed down the track. They spin their tires and smoke fills the air. This is called the **burnout**. The burnout adds melted rubber to the track surface. The melted rubber gives the cars better traction during the race.

After the burnout, the cars are backed up behind the starting line. The crews make last-second adjustments. The yellow lights blink on the **Christmas tree**. Concentration is important. A late reaction can lose the race. The green light flashes! The drivers push their accelerator pedals to the floor.

PRE-STAGE

STAGE

19

The cars are off in a deafening roar. Flames shoot from the **headers** of the funny cars. The race only lasts about five seconds. Both cars cross the finish line.

Fast FaCt

John Force is the most famous funny car racer ever. He's won 14 NHRA World Funny Car Championships.

Chutes pop open behind each car. The winning team hurries to rebuild the car's engine so it will be ready for the next race.

Glossary

burnout—the act of spinning tires before a race to heat the rubber and track for better traction

carbon fiber—a material made from mixing strong fabric with plastic; the body of a funny car is made out of carbon fiber.

chassis—the metal frame upon which a funny car is built

Christmas tree—a tower of bright yellow, green, and red lights that helps start a car race

chutes—parachutes that help cars stop at the end of a race

driveshaft—the part of a car that transfers power from the engine to the wheels

headers—the parts of an exhaust system that are attached to the engine; unlike most cars, funny car headers stick out from the car.

horsepower—a unit for measuring the power of an engine

modify—to change a vehicle to increase its performance or improve its look

nitromethane—an explosive fuel that helps power funny cars

power-to-weight ratio—an engine's horsepower divided by the weight of the car it powers

production vehicles—cars sold to the general public for use on streets and highways

supercharger—a device that mixes large amounts of air with an engine's fuel to create more power

traction—the grip of a vehicle's tires on the ground

wheelbase—the distance between the center of a car's front wheel and the center of its rear wheel on the same side

To Learn More

AT THE LIBRARY

Gigliotti, Jim. *Hottest Dragsters and Funny Cars*. Berkeley Heights, N.J.: Enslow, 2007.

Kaelberer, Angie Peterson. *Funny Cars*. Mankato, Minn.: Capstone, 2006.

Von Finn, Denny. *Dragsters*. Minneapolis, Minn.: Bellwether, 2009.

ON THE WEB

Learning more about funny cars is as easy as 1, 2, 3.

1. Go to www.factsurfer.com.

2. Enter "funny cars" into the search box.

3. Click the "Surf" button and you will see a list of related Web sites.

With factsurfer.com, finding more information is just a click away.

Index